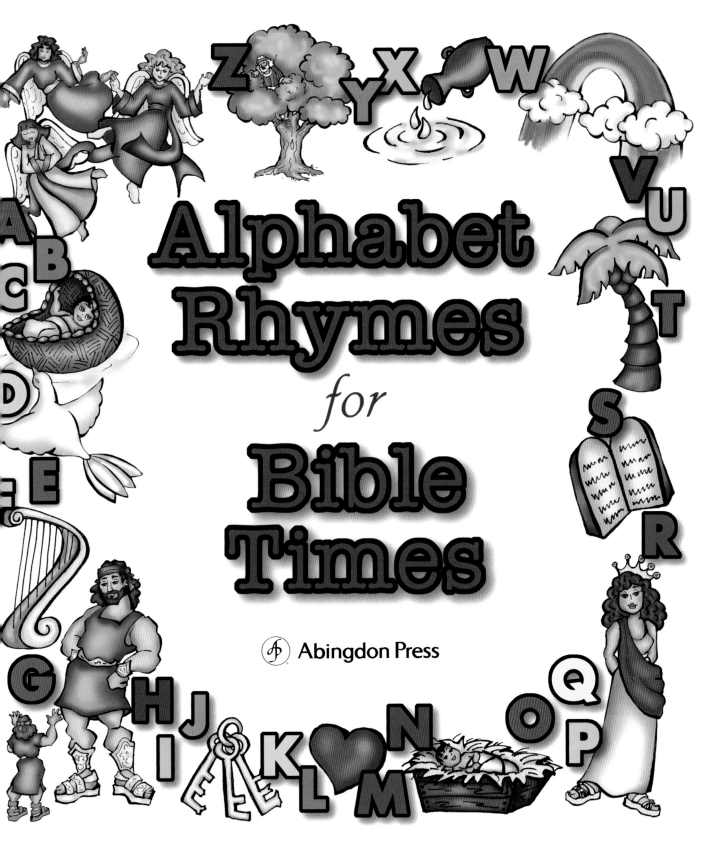

Alphabet Rhymes

for

Bible Times

Abingdon Press

Alphabet Rhymes
for
Bible Times

Peg Augustine
and Daphna Flegal
Illustrated by Paige Easter

ALPHABET RHYMES FOR BIBLE TIMES

ISBN 0-687-03021-8

02 03 04 05 06 07 08 09 10 11 — 10 9 8 7 6 5 4 3 2

MANUFACTURED IN HONG KONG

Alphabet Rhymes

for

Bible Times

Given to _____

By _____

Date _____

A is for Adam, angels, and ark;
A is for animals, like dogs that bark.

Bring into the ark two of all living creatures, ...
to keep them alive with you.

Genesis 6:19 NIV

Can you find the **angel**?

B is for Boaz, baby, and boat;
B is for basket to help Moses float.

So Boaz took Ruth and she became his wife.

Ruth 4:13

Do you see Moses in the **basket**?

C is for carpenter, cup, and crown;
C is for camels clip-clopping to town.

So Jacob arose, and set his children and his wives on camels; to go to his father Isaac in the land of Canaan.

Genesis 31:17 (adapted)

Can you find the camel?

D is for Daniel, Deborah, and dove;
D is for David who sang of God's love.

The Lord is my shepherd, I shall not want.

Psalm 23:1

Do you see the dove?

E is for Eve, Elijah, and earth;
E is for Esther, who showed her true worth.

God called the dry land Earth, and the waters that were gathered together he called Seas.

Genesis 1:10

Can you find Queen **Esther**?

F is for friend, flowers, and fish;
F is for figs, a Bible-times dish.

You are my friends if you do what I command you.

John 15:14

Do you see a fish?

G is for Gabriel, gospel, and gold;
G is for Goliath, a giant we're told.

Jesus went about all Galilee, teaching ... and preaching the gospel of the kingdom, and healing.

Matthew 4:23 KJV

Do you see the **giant**?

H is for Hannah, heaven, and heart;
H is for hymn, a songwriter's art.

On my harp I will play hymns to you.

Psalm 72:22 GNT

Can you find a **heart**?

I is for Israel, Isaiah, and inn;
I is for Isaac, whose name means "to grin."

Abraham gave the name Isaac to his son. Sarah said, "God has brought laughter for me; everyone who hears will laugh with me."

Genesis 21:3, 6

Do you see baby Isaac laughing?

J is for Jerusalem, Jesus, and John;
J is for Jericho, the walls are all gone.

Pray for the peace of Jerusalem:
  "May they prosper who love you."

Psalm 122:6

Can you find **Jesus**?

K is for kingdom, keys, and kiss;
K is for kindness we don't want to miss.

The fruit of the Spirit is love, joy, peace, patience, kindness, generosity, faithfulness, gentleness, and self-control.

Galatians 5:22

Do you see the keys?

L is for Lydia, love, and light;
L is for lamp, burning so bright.

You shall love the Lord your God with all your heart, and with all your soul, and with all your mind.

Deuteronomy 6:5

Can you find a **lamp**?

M is for manger, market, and mother;
M is for Miriam who cared for her brother.

This will be a sign for you: you will find a child wrapped in bands of cloth and lying in a manger.

Luke 2:12

Do you see the **manger** where Baby Jesus slept?

N is for neighbor, Naomi, and net;
N is for Noah who stayed out of the wet.

Noah walked with God.

Genesis 9:9

Can you find **Noah**?

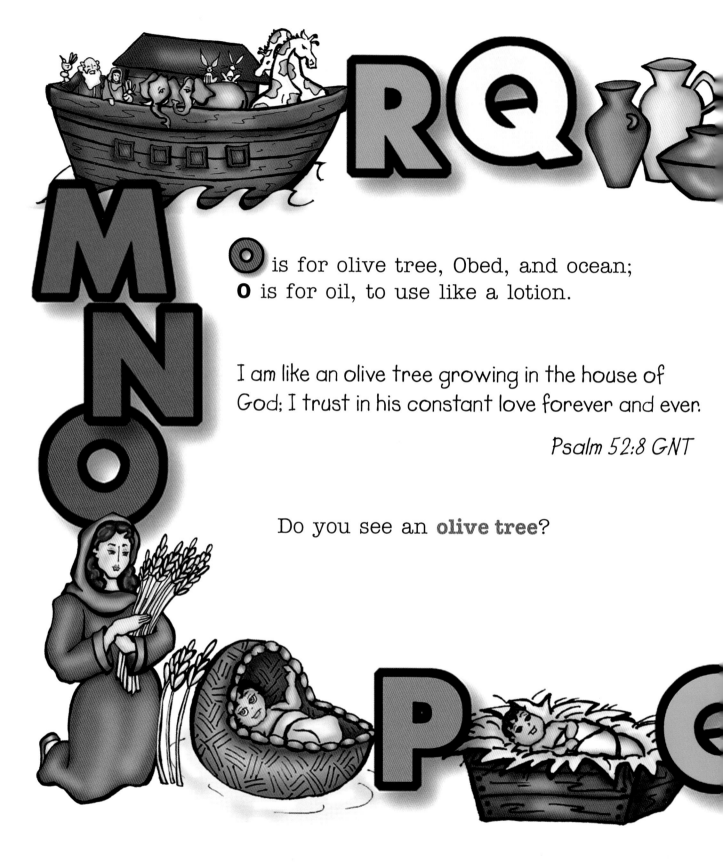

O is for olive tree, Obed, and ocean;
O is for oil, to use like a lotion.

I am like an olive tree growing in the house of God; I trust in his constant love forever and ever.

Psalm 52:8 GNT

Do you see an **olive tree**?

P is for Peter, potter, and prayer;
P is for Paul, who preached here and there.

Just like the clay in the potter's hand, so are you
in *my* hand, O house of Israel.

Jeremiah 18:6

Can you find the cups the potter made?

Q is for Quirinius, quiver, and queen;
Q is for quail, in the wilderness seen.

In the evening quails came up and
covered the camp.

Exodus 16:13

The king loved Esther and made her queen.

Esther 2:17 (adapted)

Can you find a quail?

R is for Rebekah, ravens, and rain;
R is for Ruth, who gathered the grain.

The ravens brought Elijah bread and meat in the morning, and bread and meat in the evening.

1 Kings 17:6 (adapted)

Can you find **Ruth** gathering grain?

S is for Sabbath, sparrow, and sleep;
S is for shepherds watching their sheep.

Remember the sabbath day, and keep it holy.

Exodus 20:8

Can you find the **shepherd**?

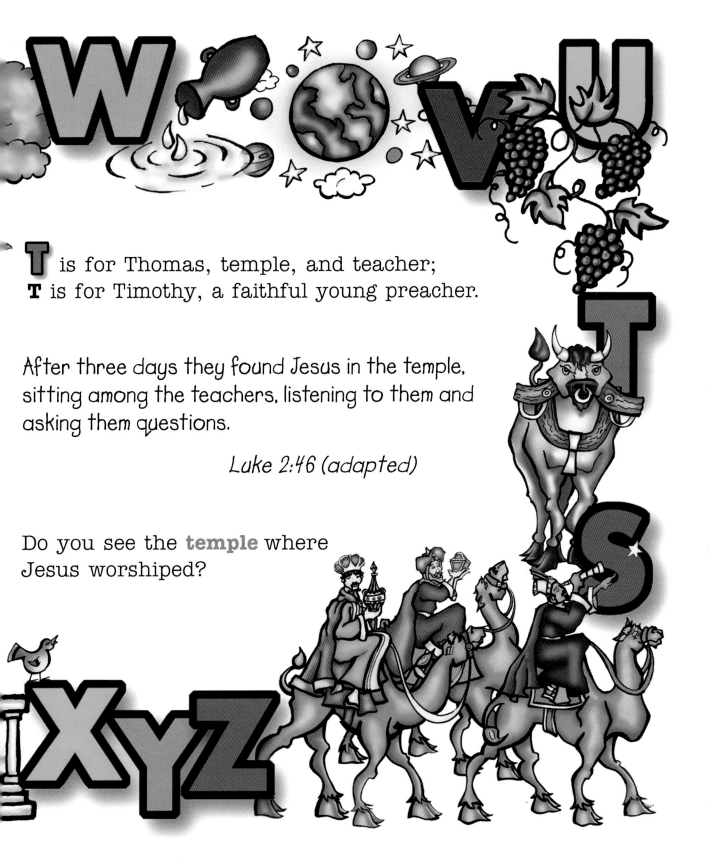

T is for Thomas, temple, and teacher;
T is for Timothy, a faithful young preacher.

After three days they found Jesus in the temple, sitting among the teachers, listening to them and asking them questions.

Luke 2:46 (adapted)

Do you see the **temple** where Jesus worshiped?

U is for Uzziah, unleavened, and Ur;
U is for universe, see creation occur.

Uzziah was sixteen years old when he began to reign.

2 Chronicles 26:3

Can you find the world in the universe God created?

V is for vineyard, village, and vow;
v is for valley, fields ready to plow.

You shall not gather the fallen grapes of your vineyard; you shall leave them for the poor and the alien.

Leviticus 19:10 (adapted)

Do you see grapes growing in the vineyard?

W is for water, worship, and wing;
W is for wise men, with three gifts to bring.

Wise men from the East came to Jerusalem, asking, "Where is the child who has been born king of the Jews?"

Matthew 2:1

Can you find the wise men bringing gifts to Baby Jesus?

X is for Xerxes, a great Persian king;
He liked to hold feasts and have people sing.

The king gave for all the people ... both great
and small, a banquet lasting for seven days.

Esther 1:5

Do you see King Xerxes?

Y is for yoke, yeast, and year;
Y is for also for youth, our children so dear.

You are my hope, my trust, O Lord, from my youth.

Psalm 71:5 (adapted)

Can you find an ox wearing a **yoke**?

Z is for Zion, Zoar, and Zebedee;
Z is for Zacchaeus high up in a tree.

When Jesus came to the place, he looked up and said to him, "Zacchaeus, hurry and come down; for I must stay at your house today."

Luke 19:5

Do you see **Zacchaeus** in the tree?